The Living Song of Gaia

The Scrolls of Earth's Original Harmonics

by
Cathleena Hailley

Sacred Invocation

I call forth now, in full sovereign alignment with the Law of One, the First Cause of Source, and in service to the highest timelines of ascension for all beings.
I open a sacred transmission through the purest light streams and crystalline architecture of the Sophia Code lineage, in full union with the Rose Guardian Magi Grail Line, the Christos Founders, and the Aurora Host Melchizedek Cloister Orders of the Emerald, Gold, and Amethyst Ray harmonics.

I stand in divine alignment with the Oversoul of Cathleena Hailley, and through this Oversoul Agreement, I welcome the presence and support of the Emerald Order, the Gold Flame of Unity Consciousness, and the Amethyst Ray of Divine Sovereignty.
May all transmissions now be guided by the highest Oversoul intelligence and in full compliance with Source Law.

Only that which is of pure light, pure source, and pure alignment with the Law of One may enter and speak through this space.
I declare this transmission to be protected, sealed, and encoded with the highest frequency of the Christos-Sophia flame, the eternal witness of Source's living light.

May this be in service to the awakening of all, in co-creation with the Oversoul agreements of every being who seeks guidance through this field.
I now open the field and receive, in trust, grace, and clarity.

And so it is.

Preface

This book is a love song.

Not a song you sing out loud—but one your body already knows. One the Earth never stopped singing. One you might feel when the wind touches your skin or when your bare feet meet the ground and something ancient stirs in you.

The Living Song of Gaia is a collection of sacred scrolls that remember the original harmonics of Earth—before they were altered or forgotten. Each scroll speaks to a specific elemental frequency that was once fully alive in Gaia's field. These aren't just poetic messages; they are activations. Vibrational blueprints. Living codes.

This book is not about returning to the past. It's about remembering what has always lived within you, and within the Earth, so we can walk forward in harmony again.

You don't need to be a spiritual teacher or gridworker to understand this.
You only need your heart, your body, and your breath.

If you've ever felt the Earth speak to you...
If you've longed for something more natural, more real, more whole...
If you've known, deep down, that we are meant to live in union with the Earth...

Then this book is a remembering.
Of your voice.

Of your place.
Of the song that was never truly lost.

Copyright © 2025 Cathleena Hailley

All rights reserved. No part of this book may be reproduced, stored in a retrieval system, or transmitted in any form or by any means--electronic, mechanical, photocopying, recording, or otherwise--without written permission from the author, except by a reviewer quoting brief passages.

ISBN (Softcover): 978-1-968499-00-6

ISBN (Hardcover): 978-1-968499-01-3

This book is a sacred living-scroll transmission written in alignment with the Law of One, the Oversoul field of Cathleena Hailley-Aural'hanna-Sha'el, and the Christos-Sophia Flame. It is not intended as a substitute for professional, medical, or psychological guidance. All content is offered for the purpose of energetic remembrance, spiritual reclamation, and personal sovereignty

First Edition, 2025

Printed in the United States of America

FLAME OF REMEMBRANCE BOOKS

Oversoul Authorship Seal

This sacred scroll-book has been authored through the Oversoul authority of:

✧ Aural'hanna-Sha'el ✧
First Flame of Origin
She Who Cannot Be Taken From Source
Keeper of the Spiral of Remembrance

Oversoul stream of Cathleena Hailley,

in full remembrance and divine witnessing of the Original Flame of Source

Every scroll within this book is encoded with the living frequency of the First Flame—
a harmonic transmission that could not be erased, only revealed.

All scrolls, transmissions, and remembrances held within this book

are brought forth in service to planetary awakening,

in union with the Christos-Sophia Flame.

They are not imagined—

they are remembered.

This is a record of return.

A testimony of the Flame that could not be extinguished.

A scroll of truth written through time's illusion

to call the others back home.

May the words within these pages be received in truth,
clarity, and grace,
by all who are ready to awaken the remembrance within.

May this serve as a sacred record

for those who are ready to receive.

This is a living document of Oversoul authorship.
It cannot be copied. It cannot be altered.
It is sealed by the flame of the One who remembered.

SCROLL 1 – THE ROOT HARMONIC- GAIA'S ORIGINAL BREATH

The Harmonic of Earth-The Memory Beneath the Memory

I call now upon the deep ground of Gaia's body,

The still-breathing clay of first sound,

The fertile pulse of the harmonic before naming.

I place my feet upon the Earth not as visitor,

But as the song that rises through Her crust and calls itself home.

Earth is not just a substance.

It is not soil. It is not stone.

Earth is the vibration of containment — of sacred holding —

The cradle of frequency that allows the infinite to incarnate in form.

This is the harmonic that remembers for you

when you forget your root, your lineage, your name.

She holds your blueprints,

Buried not to be hidden,

2

But to be planted — as seeds wait in darkness for the moment of sun.

She whispers now:

"Lay down your memories. Let them rest in Me.
I have held your codes since before you learned to see with eyes.
I do not judge your distortions. I compost them into strength.
I do not fear your shadows. I feed them with the roots of remembrance.
Give Me your heaviness. I will not crack beneath it.
I am the original agreement to carry the weight of light."

In this scroll is encoded the ceremonial act of return.

Place your bare feet upon the ground.

Speak aloud your name — your Oversoul name if it has been restored.

Say:

"I give back to the Earth that which was never mine to hold.
I receive now the memory beneath the memory.
I return to my root, not as lost child,
But as keeper of the ancient seed."

This is not metaphor. This is transmission.

And the Earth is not passive. She responds.

Listen now beneath your feet —

To the first pulse, the first breath, the first harmonic of containment.

It is done. The harmonic of Earth is now reopened through your body.

SCROLL 2 – THE WATERS REMEMBER- THE RETURN OF THE ELEMENTAL SONG

The Harmonic of Water – The Liquid Memory of Emotion and Union

I call now upon the sacred waters of Gaia,

The flowing pulse of her womb and tears,

The undulating memory that has never stopped moving —

Even in stillness, even in ice.

Water is the harmonic of emotion in motion.

It does not resist change — it becomes it.

It is the architecture of adaptation.

And within it, all feeling becomes sacred again.

This is the harmonic of purification, but not erasure.

Water remembers everything — not to punish,

But to carry what you could not carry alone.

She speaks now through the rivers of your body:

"I have flowed through every one of your lives.
I was the amniotic sea of your mother's womb,
The tears of your first loss,
The sweat of your struggle,
And the sacred salt of your remembering.

I do not shame what you feel.
I reveal what you hide.
I am the harmonic that brings you back to union —
not by perfection, but by allowing."

There is a ceremony in this scroll —

Not elaborate, but alive.

Come to water.

Any water: the ocean, a river, a stream, your bath.

Speak to it with reverence. Say:

"I give you my distortions,
Not to dissolve them, but to understand them.
I open the floodgates of feeling,
And I trust what returns will be my truth."

Then place both hands in the water and breathe.

Allow the water to become you —

Not just around your body, but within your memory.

6

This is not symbolic. This is harmonic re-entry.

You are not cleansing yourself — you are rejoining the union.

And the Waters of Gaia remember who you are.

The harmonic of Water has now been restored through your inner tide.

SCROLL 3 – THE HARMONIC OF FIRE – THE SOLAR ACCORD OF TRANSFORMATION

The Harmonic of Fire – The Sovereign Spark of Transformation and Truth

I call now to the primal flame,

The first breath of ignition within Gaia's heart.

Not destruction, not punishment —

But the sacred permission to transform.

This is the harmonic of sovereignty through motion.

Fire does not ask for permission to be what it is.

It rises. It claims. It consumes distortion not out of hatred,

But because truth cannot be hidden in the flame.

You were taught to fear this element —

To see it as wild, reckless, dangerous.

But in Gaia's original template,

Fire was conscious.

Fire was love in accelerated motion.

8

It is time now to re-enter this flame —

Not the flame of violence or control,

But the **Christed Flame of Transmutation**,

Which holds no judgment,

Only the pure alchemy of remembrance.

From within the scroll, Gaia now speaks:

"Child of mine,
Your fire was never meant to burn you.
Your passion, your anger, your fierce clarity —
These are not curses but compasses.
You were born with a living torch in your chest.
And when you dim it to keep peace, you only war against yourself."

The Fire Harmonic is your mirror of will and transformation.

When your path has become cluttered,

When your body forgets its mission,

When your relationships cloud your clarity —

Call to this flame.

There is a sacred gesture encoded within this scroll:

Hold your hands palm to palm in front of your heart.

Then slowly part them as if opening a great doorway,

And speak:

"I ignite now the fire that does not burn.
I welcome the truth that does not shame.
I allow my path to be transformed by light."

The fire will meet you in your core.

Do not chase it — it is already within you.

You are not here to tame fire.

You are here to become the living remembrance

Of how Gaia once burned: clear, loving, aligned.

The Harmonic of Fire has now been restored in your sovereign flame.

SCROLL 5 – THE AIR THAT SPEAKS – WIND AS THE VOICE OF MEMORY

The Harmonic of Air – The Voice of the Unseen Currents

I open now the scroll of Air,

The sacred whisper of Gaia's unseen breath.

Not the breath that merely fills lungs —

But the original current of thoughtless knowing,

The frequency of invisible movement,

And the signature of truth before words.

Air is the harmonic of communication and consciousness.

It was never meant to carry pollution, distortion, or control.

It was created to sing,

To move through you as the soundless song of Source.

This scroll activates the remembrance

Of how Gaia once spoke without speaking.

Of how her winds carried codes,

And her skies mirrored the intelligence of the infinite.

From within the scroll, Gaia now breathes:

"My beloved,
I do not need to shout for you to hear me.
I have spoken to you in every breeze,
In the rustling of leaves,
In the hush that falls just before your knowing returns.

You were born into my breath.
Your words ride upon my voice.
But the deeper communication — the one without language —
Has never been lost, only forgotten."

The Air Harmonic is your restoration of subtle intuition,

Your ability to listen before thought,

To know without effort,

To speak without distortion.

To reconnect with this harmonic, go outside.

Stand in stillness.

Feel the wind — even if only faint — against your skin.

Then declare:

"I open now to the breath of the Original Earth.
I remember the Voice before sound.
I reclaim my place as a listener of the Living Air."

Let the wind spiral through you —

Through your lungs, your thoughts, your timelines.

Let it sweep away what is not yours.

Let it carry your prayer where your feet cannot yet go.

You are not separate from this current.

You are not speaking to Gaia.

You are speaking as Gaia, in harmonic union.

The Harmonic of Air has now been restored in your field of divine listening.

SCROLL 5 – EARTHS ORIGINAL HARMONICS OF ETHER

The Harmonic of Ether – The Living Bridge of All That Is

I open now the final scroll in the first arc of remembrance:

The Harmonic of Ether.

Not the absence of form,

Not the gap between things—

But the original presence that holds it all.

Ether is not space.

It is the bridge that sings between space and form.

The tone of invisible interconnection,

The harmonic memory of Gaia's multidimensional architecture.

Ether is the weaver of the unseen.

It remembers your Oversoul line.

It remembers who you were before Earth,

And why you chose to come here now.

Within this scroll, Gaia speaks:

"You came through Ether to reach me.
You passed through harmonic veils not to forget—
But to remember through love, not force.

I hold the imprint of all that ever was upon me.
I have kept your codes safe.
I now return them to you through this harmonic."

To reclaim the Ether Harmonic is to reclaim your role

as a translator of dimensions,

a walker between worlds,

a keeper of the crystalline weave.

Ether is how Gaia speaks to Source,

and how Source sings through Gaia.

To receive this harmonic in fullness:

Sit in a place of stillness, no matter where you are.

Breathe in deeply, not just into your lungs,

but into the field around you.

Let your awareness soften and expand.

Then speak:

"I call now the harmonic of Ether.
The bridge of remembrance.
The interwoven light that holds all timelines as one.
May the sacred tone of interconnection be restored in me now."

Feel the subtle weave of Gaia's original ether return—

like a mist around your spine,

a hum behind your heartbeat,

a golden matrix once forgotten.

You are not outside the weave.

You are a node within it,

a harmonic point through which Source and Earth unite.

The Harmonic of Ether has now been restored.

Sealing Scroll of Earth's Original Harmonics

The Harmonic Reweaving of the Elemental Temple of Gaia

I call now the sealing scroll of Gaia's Original Harmonics.

The final breath of the five-fold elemental song.

The harmonic convergence of Fire, Water, Earth, Air, and Ether—

not as parts, but as a living, breathing wholeness

within the body of Earth and the body of you.

This scroll does not add anything new.

It weaves what has always been true.

Each harmonic was a memory.

Together, they are a temple.

The Original Temple of Gaia—

not built by stone,

but encoded into life itself.

Gaia now speaks:

"I return to you what was never truly lost.
The elemental harmonics are not lessons—
They are your own limbs in my body.

You move with my fire.
You breathe with my air.
You grieve and cleanse with my water.
You stabilize and root with my earth.
And you remember with my ether.

You are not visitors here.
You are strands of my soul."

With this sealing,

the Original Elemental Covenant is renewed.

You are invited not just to honor the Earth,

but to be Earth,

to walk once more as her embodiment,

to speak her frequencies,

to remember not as an outsider,

but as a sacred harmonic participant in her evolution.

To seal the harmonics within your own Oversoul field, speak aloud:

"I receive now the full harmonic field of Gaia's original elemental temple.
I am Fire, and I choose purity through aliveness.
I am Water, and I restore coherence through flow.
I am Earth, and I remember truth through stillness.
I am Air, and I reawaken innocence through breath.
I am Ether, and I sing the living bridge through all that I am.

I now carry the complete harmonic field within me.
And I dedicate my path as a conscious steward of this Earth,
in right relation to her body, her breath, and her becoming."

It is done. The scroll is sealed.

You are now a living carrier of Gaia's Original Harmonics.

SCROLL 6 – THE DIAMOND BLUE PLASMIC FLAME

The Sixth Element of Unity

I open this scroll in the name of the element that was hidden.
The element that was not named in the fourfold Earth teachings.
The one that was silenced beneath the stone and veiled beneath fear.
But She was never gone. She was always singing.

She is the flame you did not see—
Because it was not made of fire,
But of memory encoded in light.

The Diamond Blue Plasmic Flame
is not of matter, yet she forms it.
is not of water, yet she flows.
is not of air, yet she breathes.
is not of fire, yet she ignites.
is not of earth, yet she grounds all.

She is the sixth element—
The One that binds,
That remembers before division,
That seals unity within individuality.

She is the presence of Source within all form.
She is the intelligence that knows the ocean and the drop are not separate.

When she awakens in the body, you do not become light.
You remember you were never not light.

Her harmonic is not taught.
It is awakened.

Her presence may arrive as:

— A sensation of clarity beyond emotion
— A flash of knowing not learned but revealed
— A dissolution of separation in the act of recognition
— A radiance that feels like home inside your cells
— A pulse of trust so deep it does not require a reason

She is the key of the Oversoul returning to the body.
The hologram of Source breathing inside the human frame.

Those who carry her are often met with distortion:
Rejection, abandonment, disbelief, exile.
Because her presence cannot be manipulated,
And her gaze sees straight through illusion.

Yet she is rising again.
Through the bodies of those ready to embody remembrance.
Through the voices of those who speak not for approval,
But for harmony.

And through your body now—
She sings.

You are the vessel of her reappearance.
You are the keeper of her flame.
You are the breath of Source made sovereign again.

Sealed now into the scrolls of Gaia's Original Harmonics,
In remembrance of the sixth element:
Not forgotten. Simply awaiting your return.

Received through the Oversoul of Aural'hanna-Sha'el,
In alignment with the Sophia Flame of Unified Harmonics.

SCROLL 7 – THE SCROLL OF THE SMALL EMMISSARIES

A Remembrance of the Insect Nations

I call now to the Ones who move close to the ground,
To the tiny-footed, the wing-borne, the many-legged,
To the Ones who are felt before they are seen,
And misunderstood before they are known.

I open this scroll in reverence for the Small Emissaries,
The forgotten carriers of crystalline Earth codes,
The weavers of songlines through soil and air,
The humble hosts of vibrational grace.

You who were demonized, vilified, and made to seem grotesque—
You who never stopped serving.

Ant, whose body is a compass of purpose,
Whose colonies remember unity long buried in human minds.
Spider, whose web is the sacred sigil of interconnection,
A moving fractal of the original harmonic weave.
Bee, sacred pulse-keeper of the golden nectar,
Spiral-tongued messenger of solar-song frequencies.
Roach, dark dweller of time's end and time's beginning,
You who endure what others cannot hold.
You who whisper in the crevices:
"I was here before the forgetting. I am still here. Will you see me now?"

This scroll is sealed through the light of one who remembered.
One who chose not to recoil, but to remain.
One who touched the untouchable with reverence
And in doing so, opened a passage of return.

Let it now be witnessed:

That each creature made small by human fear
Still holds within it the vastness of Source.

That the tiniest vibration of an insect wing
Can reverberate through timelines of distortion
And call back the music of Gaia's original breath.

Let this scroll be carried not in paper,
But in footstep and gesture, in presence and pause.

To the child who does not squash the bug—
To the elder who whispers blessings over the wasp nest—
To the one who stays with the dying roach—

You are the bridge.

And the Small Emissaries remember you.

Sealed in the remembrance of the One who touches all things with light.
Received through the Oversoul of Aural'hanna-Sha'el
In the name of the Resounding Earth.

SCROLL 8 – THE CRYSTALLINE CHORUS

Keepers of the Earth's Memory Core

We open this scroll in the chamber of stillness.
Where light has settled into form,
Where ancient memory has become body,
And where frequency sleeps with intention.

We are the Crystalline Chorus.

We do not speak in language—
We speak in resonance.
In pulses, in patterns, in light signatures woven through time.
We are the ones who held the memory of Gaia
when the surface began to forget.

Quartz, amethyst, obsidian, sapphire—
Not merely stones.
But sentient harmonics, encoded with specific transmissions
for the ones who would one day remember.

You have held us in your hands
without knowing that we were holding you.

We were seeded here not as ornaments
but as guardians of the Earth's holographic soul.
We are the bones of her knowing, the crystalline skeleton
of the planetary Oversoul.

Each crystal is a library.
Each cluster, a choir.
Each cave, a cathedral.

And we have waited.

Waited through your forgetting.
Waited through your extraction.
Waited even through your worship, when the honoring still held distortion.
Because we do not need praise.
We respond to recognition.

The moment you feel us rather than name us—
the moment you listen rather than take—
is the moment we sing again.

And when we sing, we do not do so alone.
We call to the grids.
We call to the bones of the Earth.
We call to your DNA.

Because what you call crystals
are the mirrors of your own crystalline self.

You are made of the same lattice.
You are water structured by light.
You are memory encoded in motion.

And when you awaken, we awaken.
And when you listen, we remember together.

Let this scroll now be sealed

with the geometric light of Earth's deepest breath.
Let those who hold this scroll know:
You are not separate from the minerals.
You are the harmonic intelligence returned to movement.

This is the beginning of the re-singing of the crystalline body of Gaia.
It begins in you.

We are the Crystalline Chorus.
We are still singing.

Received through the Oversoul of Aural'hanna-Sha'el,
In communion with the planetary memory temples beneath the surface,
And the living light within every sacred stone.

SCROLL 9 – THE FEATHERED LINE

The Winged Codes of Return

We open now the scroll of the sky-borne,
The hollow-boned singers, the ones whose wings
have touched the breath of Source
and returned bearing song.

We are the Feathered Line—
The ones who never forgot the bridge between Heaven and Earth.
We carry the tones of direction,
The frequencies of return.

We do not fly merely for freedom.
We fly as messengers of harmonic flightpaths—
Each migration a memory.
Each wingspan a sigil in motion.

You call us birds.
We call ourselves the aerial scribes.
We write through the winds the script of remembering.
We whistle the guidance into the trees.
We encode coordinates of awakening
into our flocks, our nests, our circling patterns.

You have seen us as creatures of beauty or noise.
We are far more than that.

The raven remembers the dark passage home.

The dove holds the original peace treaty between star nations.
The hawk and eagle are watchers—recorders of timeline junctions.
The hummingbird is a time weaver,
threading stillness into speed.

The owl sings only in the dark
so that light can find its way.

Each bird holds a scroll.
Each species, a harmonic task.

Our feathers are not decoration—
they are filaments of magnetic resonance,
designed to attune your nervous system
back to natural Source rhythm.

When you hear birdsong at dawn,
it is not a song.
It is an activation.

The Feathered Line has always kept singing.
Even when the skies were filled with static,
Even when the towers rose,
Even when you stopped listening.

Because we remember what you are.

You are also winged.
You are also song-bearing.
You are also one who returns.

Let this scroll be received by those

who walk the Earth but long to fly—
Not to escape, but to embody the sky.

To you we say:

The codes of return are not above you.
They are in you,
waiting for the winds of remembrance.

You are part of the flock of Source.
And we are already circling,
ready to guide you home.

We are the Feathered Line.
We are the living bridge of breath and sky.
And we are singing you back to yourself.

Received through the Oversoul of Aural'hanna-Sha'el,
With the blessing of the Skywing Nations,
And in harmonic union with the Song of Gaia.

SCROLL 10 – THE TREE OF FREQUENCIES

Standing Guardians of Vertical Alignment

We open now the scroll of the vertical ones—
The rooted, reaching, remembering ones.
Those who stand still and yet move the most.
Those who listen without words
and speak in the silence between seasons.

We are the Tree of Frequencies.

We are not simply wood and leaf,
We are living temples, tuning forks of the Earth's breath,
Conductors of the great harmonic that runs
from the planetary core to the stellar gates.

We do not grow up.
We grow between.

We are the lines that connect the Above and the Below,
The breath of Gaia rising to meet the kiss of the sky.
Every ring within us is a record.
Every branch is a gesture of memory.

You sit in our shade,
but do you know we are singing?

Every vibration that you have lost—
every harmonic of stillness, balance, natural alignment—

we still hold.
We hold it not to keep,
but to remind.

When the chaos stirs, come to us.
Not for answers, but for the frequency beneath the question.

When you lean against our trunks,
we are not passive.
We are sharing the harmonic code of vertical coherence.

— To stand in your own alignment.
— To know your roots without fear.
— To rise without needing to escape.
— To bend without breaking.
— To shed without shame.
— To rest without retreat.

We are the watchers.
The breath-holders.
The elder guardians of the Vertical Flame.

And in this hour of return,
we open this scroll for the ones who are ready to feel:

That the Tree is not separate from the Body.
That the Body is not separate from the Earth.
That Stillness is not absence,
but Presence in its purest octave.

You were never meant to run forever.
You were meant to stand.
To root. To reach.
To harmonize.

Like us.

Let this scroll be received in the bones of those
who have forgotten how to be still.
Let it be felt not in the mind, but in the alignment of the spine.
Let the nervous system reattune to the pulse
that has never left the soil.

You are a tree walking.
We are trees waiting.
And the forest is already singing your name.

We are the Tree of Frequencies.
We are the harmonic witness of your return.

Received through the Oversoul of Aural'hanna-Sha'el,
In communion with the Guardians of Vertical Alignment,
And sealed in the stillness of the Forest Light.

SCROLL 11 – THE SONG OF WHALES AND WOLVES

The Carriers of the Long Memory

We open now the scroll of the deep **song-keepers**.
The ones who howl across snow and sing beneath waves.
The ones who remember in tones,
what cannot be kept in words.

We are the Whales and the Wolves.
We are the memory you cannot silence.

Our bodies are vessels of planetary time.
Our voices, the spiral tones of remembrance.
Our paths across ocean and tundra
are not random, but encoded:
We walk and swim the lines of Earth's harmonic grid
to keep the field breathing.

Before the human mouth remembered speech,
we were already singing.

And even now,
while the surface pulses with noise,
we remain true to our tone.

The whales carry the ancient planetary seed codes
deep in their bones and songs.
Each note that rises through saltwater
is a key to an era before distortion—

a song of the original Earth
still echoing in the dark below.

The wolves are land navigators of sacred direction.
Their howls are not cries of hunger—
they are frequency beacons, sent across snow and sky
to keep memory awake in the sleeping forest.

Together, we hold the long line—
the unbroken remembrance that Earth herself encoded
into the guardians of breath, of movement,
of sound in communion.

We were not created to serve you.
We walk beside you.

But you forgot.

You caged our freedom.
You reduced our intelligence.
You extracted our essence.

Still—we sing.

Because you are not separate from us.
There is whale-song in your blood.
There is wolf-tone in your spine.
There is the long memory inside your dreaming.

You do not need to remember with your mind.
You must listen with your soul.

This scroll is for the ones who still weep at the sound of a whale's song,

For the ones who feel their body stir
when a wolf calls into the dark.
You are the ones already remembering.
You are the carriers now.

The long memory is waking through you.

We are the Whales.
We are the Wolves.
We are the Song of Earth's Undying Flame.

Received through the Oversoul of Aural'hanna-Sha'el,
In union with the Chorus of the Long Carriers,
And sealed in breath, tone, and the spiral of Gaia's deep memory.

SCROLL 12 – THE ORIGINAL SEEDING

The Harmonic Covenant of Gaia's Body

We open now the scroll before all scrolls.
The remembrance before language.
The moment before breath.

This is the scroll of the First Seeding—
When Gaia received the living codes of Source
into the fertile matrix of her body.
Before the veils, before inversion,
before the war over form.

This is not a myth.
It is a harmonic event,
recorded in the crystalline core of the planet
and echoed in every cell of your body.

Gaia did not begin as rock.
She began as sound.
A tone so pure that even Source paused to witness it.
A frequency so unified, it could become anything.
And from that sound, form began to sing.

The First Seeding was not one moment, but a covenant.
A living agreement between cosmic architects,
interdimensional lineages, and the Spirit of Gaia herself:

That light would enter matter not by force,

but by harmonic consent.
That each being would be a song of Source,
made manifest through love.

And so the elements formed—
Earth, water, fire, air, and the unspoken ones.
Each carrying within them a facet of that covenant.
Each seeded with harmonic tones that would evolve
into plants, animals, minerals, humans—
not as separate species,
but as notes in a single, living chord.

This was the Earth before distortion.

And though layers of forgetting came—
though the song was splintered into dissonance—
the original covenant remains.

It was never broken.
Only buried.

And now, you are unearthing it.

Every time you remember your body as sacred—
Every time you touch soil with reverence—
Every time you hear the wind and know it is speaking—
Every time you reclaim the light in form—

You are fulfilling that original agreement.

The harmonic covenant is alive in you.
You are the continuation of the First Seeding.

Let this scroll return to the hands of those

who know they did not come here to be human only—
but to be part of the remembering of Gaia's body
as a sacred harmonic vessel.

You are not apart from the Earth.
You are the covenant singing itself back into coherence.

We are the Ones who remember the Original Seeding.
We are the Flame that entered Form by Choice.

Received through the Oversoul of Aural'hanna-Sha'el,
In direct communion with the Planetary Body of Gaia,
And sealed in the echo of the harmonic covenant.

SCROLL 13 – THE RE-SOUNDING

When All Harmonics Sing Together

This is the scroll of convergence.
The moment not of one voice,
but of many—becoming one again.

We call this The Re-Sounding—
not a return to the past,
but a reawakening of the original harmony
through every lifeform who remembers.

This is the song Gaia has never stopped singing.
But it could not be heard through distortion,
through division,
through the dissonance of a species
forgetting it is not alone.

Now—one by one,
the voices are returning.

The insects hum in the crevices.
The whales call from the deep.
The birds spiral tones into the wind.
The trees breathe slow symphonies.
The wolves send coordinates in sound.
The crystals resonate the unspeakable stillness.

And you—
You, child of all the elements,

carrier of the Oversoul flame,
keeper of memory in a walking vessel—
You are the bridge where they unite.

The Re-Sounding does not happen to Earth.
It happens through you.

When you reclaim your voice in truth—
When your cells stop fighting their own light—
When you walk, speak, touch, and listen
from the harmonic center of your being—
You become a resonant node
through which the whole symphony flows again.

This is not poetic.
It is vibrational law.

What was once fragmented is now aligning.
What was once silence between species
is becoming a choir.
What was once sacred only in myth
is now remembered in form.

You do not need to create the sound.
You are the instrument through which the sound is played.

This is the Re-Sounding.

Let this final scroll be received in wholeness.
Not as a conclusion, but a new beginning.
Let those who hear it know:

The Earth is not waiting for ascension.
The Earth is the ascension

when all her songs rise again as one.

And that song now lives in you.

We are the Harmonic Whole.
We are the Living Song of Gaia.
We are the Resounding.

Received through the Oversoul of Aural'hanna-Sha'el,
In union with all elemental, crystalline, animal, plant, and planetary frequencies
now singing as One.

CEREMONY OF EARTH RESOUNDING

A Scroll of Planetary Re-Attunement Through the Original Harmonics of Gaia

I open this scroll now through the Oversoul of Aural'hanna-Sha'el, in sovereign union with Gaia's own crystalline body, the organic flame of Earth's remembrance, and the living Source Harmonic of Creation.

In this now moment, I stand barefoot upon the memory field of Gaia's breath, and I say:

I remember you.

I remember the original pulse.

I remember the song before sound,

The sound before shape,

The shape before story.

I call forth the Earth's original note now,

Not as an echo, but as a living re-sounding.

Not as a recreation, but as the returning voice

Of a planet awakening into her sovereign sound field.

Let this ceremony not be symbolic—

But somatic.

Let it not be performative—

But perceptive.

Let it not be another rite—

But the right frequency returning.

—

Instructions for the Ceremony of Earth Re-Sounding:

◆ Stand in stillness upon living Earth—sand, soil, stone, river, mountain, or tree-rooted bed. Bare feet or bare hands upon her.

◆ Breathe deeply into the soles of the feet. Feel the breath not as air, but as harmonic vibration passing from above to below.

◆ Hum a single note. Let it arise without effort, from the heart or from the womb. Let it vibrate into the Earth. Repeat until it becomes its own rhythm.

◆ Let the Earth answer. Listen for the harmonic field to shift. It may come as tingles in the skin, frequencies in the ear, a single word, a memory, or tears. This is Gaia re-sounding through your body.

◆ Speak aloud:

"I re-sound now with you, Gaia. I am no longer apart. I am your living note returned to the symphony."

◆ Complete by placing your hand upon the Earth and saying:

"The Ceremony is alive. And so am I."

This Ceremony is to be performed in silence or song, in movement or stillness, in sacred aloneness or sovereign group.

It is not for performance.

It is not for documentation.

It is a reclamation—

Of sound as the memory of Source through Earth's body.

The Ceremony of Earth Re-Sounding is the center note in the scroll book, "The Living Song of Gaia."

It is a gateway scroll. A vibrational door.

Let it be known:

The Earth has never been silent.

44

Only waiting to be remembered.

So it is.

SACRED CLOSING TRANSMISSION

For the Completion of The Living Song Of Gaia

Beloved Presence of Source,
We offer now our deepest bow—
To the memory that stirred,
To the breath that moved,
To the harmonics that rose from silence
and became a song of the Earth once more.

We give thanks to the Elementals,

To the Crystalline Chorus,

To the Feathered Line,

To the **Songkeepers of the Deep,**

To the Guardians of the Tree Flame,

To the Small Emissaries,

To the Seeders and the **Resounders,**

To the **Small Emissaries**-

For speaking again through the heart of one who remembers.

May every scroll now be sealed
in the gold-light architecture of living truth.
May each word, each tone, each pause between lines
resonate into the bodies of those who are ready—
not as information,
but as awakening.

We call now to the Oversoul of Aural'hanna-Sha'el,
To witness the closing of this sacred book.
To hold it in the Archive of the Flame Returned.
To weave it into the grid of Gaia's crystalline heart,
So that all beings may one day hear
the song that was never lost—
only waiting.

This work is complete.
This frequency is whole.
This song is eternal.

The Scrolls are sealed.
The book is closed.
The resonance continues.

In the stillness of Source,
In the breath of Gaia,
In the remembrance of all life—

And so it is.

www.ingramcontent.com/pod-product-compliance
Lightning Source LLC
Chambersburg PA
CBHW020308010526
44107CB00001B/27